Did That Really Happen?

Errol Dunn

Did That Really Happen?

Did That Really Happen?
ISBN 978 1 76041 907 3
Copyright © Errol Dunn 2020
Illustrations: Nathan Dunn

First published 2020 by
GINNINDERRA PRESS
PO Box 3461 Port Adelaide 5015
www.ginninderrapress.com.au

Contents

A Lifetime of Happenings…		7
1	A Bowl of Cherries	9
2	Health & Getting Well and Truly (Older, That Is)	13
3	Tall Stories, Rumours & Old Yarns	22
4	For Charitable and Community Purposes	34
5	Work Is Not All Work	41
6	The Proper and Effective Use of Fireworks	52
7	Kids Should Be Seen and Heard	57
8	Retirement, Ageing and Other Forms of Self-destruction	68

A Lifetime of Happenings, Reflective Thoughts and Ravings of a VUP (Very Unimportant Person)

This book is a brief collection of some of the humorous anecdotes from the workplace, the drinking place, the living place and a lot of other places.

All information in this book is from sources and recollections considered to be trustworthy and reliable. However, no warranty is made to the accuracy thereof.

1

A Bowl of Cherries

I don't fully subscribe to the philosophy behind the 1930s Brown and Henderson hit song 'Life is Just a Bowl of Cherries', but the first refrain below does warrant thinking about.

> 'Life is just a bowl of cherries
> Don't take it serious; it's too mysterious
> You work, you save, you worry so
> But you can't take your dough when you go, go, go.'

Maybe a verse reflecting the recognition of the humour that is around us every day would have been worthy of inclusion. However, the last line on the lyric probably covers that: 'So, live and laugh at it all.'

Don't get me wrong, please, I'm not a jabbering jester skipping down life's pathway without any serious concern for the present state or the future for my wife and family or for that of our dedicated friends.

Conversely, being too serious about it is a contagious and very debilitating disease.

Like many others, I have suffered many significant setbacks in life, had many momentous disappointments, experienced many problems. Some are still not completely resolved and, being a realist, I expect more tribulations to hit me between the eyes in the future. Nevertheless, I believe my scope of life is also broad enough to include the recognition of the more humorous side of the time we have on Earth.

I have never thought of myself as a humorously entertaining person.

I love a good witty conversation and think I can almost hold my own there on most commonplace subjects, but I don't grasp any riveting attention in leading a story or yarn telling in person.

Psychologists have been studying humour and the effects on humans of all types, of all ages and in all situations, for many centuries and there is a lot of work still out there for them to suss out.

There are many types of so called humour practised, applauded and approved by people and some of it completely escapes me as a likely member of a positively responding audience. Some types that I do loathe are mentioned below. I don't know the correct titles if there are any – these are just my titles.

I despise Self-applauding Humour, where the person tries just too damn hard to be funny. I'm sure you know the type. They either tell a bad joke or make some smart-arse quip and then immediately burst into forced raucous laughter at the end. Is it that they seriously don't understand the basics of humour? Did they miss out on getting even a smidgeon of the humour gene at birth? Or are they so desperate for attention that they do this hoping someone will feel sorry for them and laugh with them out of sympathy, thereby providing the required accolade they desire? I have no idea how it works and I'll leave that to the psychologists to wrestle with.

Then there is Tyrannical Humour, where the teller's position or standing effectively demands an appreciative response. An example: my work experiences included a company owner I once worked under, who at staff social gatherings delighted in telling lurid sick political jokes about prominent members of the political party opposite to the one he supported. His strong inference that all attending staff should laugh with him wasn't all that successful, with usually less than half the group responding feebly to his wishes. His so-called jokes were just not humorous. They might have got a giggle in the Year 6 school playground, but I doubt even that. Not to give up on his continual attempt at fame and recognition in the political jokes department, at our national conference one year he had a virtual library of the same tasteless jokes drawn up in cartoons and we endured up to two hours of a PowerPoint session of him screening and laughing at them.

The Constant Chortle Humour is where the teller continually giggles throughout the telling of their joke or story in a low voice. The worst of these teller types can also emit a fine spray of spittle at significant parts in the telling, creating a 'spider and the fly' effect where the audience person comes closer to hear and appreciate the gist of the joke or story, then gets spat on.

I love the quick, witty off the cuff responses. The American hillbilly comedy duo entertainers Homer & Jethro back in the sixties had a line on one of their live performances for an audience member who was noticeably slow picking up clever one-liners by regularly applauding late. As late as when they were into the start of the next part of the routine. Their response was, 'Lady, you watch everybody else, and when they start to applaud, you just join in.'

Or another artist I heard at a live club show once experiencing a similarly slow but loud male responder in the front row. After many interruptions from this rude baboon, the comedian asked from the stage, 'Sir, why don't we get you a notebook, you jot down what you missed in the show and maybe after we finish, we can workshop your notes with you in the quiet of the car park.'

Another one for the slow, interjecting audience member from a comedian in his live show: 'Lady, why don't you just stand up. Maybe somebody will recognise you and take you home, as it must be way past your bedtime.'

Life may not always directly relate to a bowl of cherries, but I do applaud real-life humour – things that really happened. That is what this book is about: real-life humour, according to the real world.

Given my experience over this lifetime, I have enumerated quite a number of incidents, happenings, reiterated stories and other observations that I have stitched together into this book.

Some of the work incidents documented here I have borrowed from my recent book, *Managers, Monarchs, Moralists, Mongrels and Morons,* which relates my history in the Australian electricity supply industry and my opinions on why it is in the current mess it is. The stories I have repeated here are applicable to both publications.

The title of this book emanates from the responses given by people who have read some of the reported incidents in an early draft.

I am thankful for those people who have contributed through their behaviours and experiences. Whether such contributions are the result of stupid, careless, clever, cute or otherwise behaviour, each of them is a gold-plated gem of humanity to me.

I am also so very thankful for my still reasonably crisp recollection of these events, in that I'm able to relate them here.

2

Health & Getting Well and Truly (Older, That Is)

Apart from my childhood, when I seemed to pick up any nasty bug that was going around, I have been fortunate to have enjoyed reasonably good health from my teenage years till now, where I'm in the status of 'the elderly'.

When doctors or other medical type people now treat me for something totally unrelated to age – like a dose of the flu, a gash on the hand – they all seem to say, 'Well now, at your age you need to start taking things easy.'

Recently, I had pulled a muscle in my bum (officially it's the gluteus maximus muscle, I believe) from a gardening strain and the first advice the physio said was, 'Well now, at your age…'

How come when I was twenty years younger I recall I damaged what was somewhere close to the same muscle on the other side of the body and I was given the same advice from a different medical person and told, 'Well now, at your age…you need to start to take things easy.'

I am also reminded of a time when I damaged my back at work way back when I was about nineteen years old and the doctor told me I needed to take it a bit easier and build the body up a bit more before I tried that sort of work again. 'Wait till you're a bit more developed,' was the intent. I remember this slur well, as although I was a slightly built person, I thought I was more than reasonably fit at the time – but this medical comment dashed that opinion.

Where is this free area, this perfect window? Seems I'm either too old, too young, too skinny or now I'm fully expecting if I have another medical episode, to be told by some medical person that I'm too overweight as the contributing factor. I can hear it now: 'Well now, at your age, you should be watching your weight more.'

My weight or mass to height ratio or body mass index (BMI) is about normal. However, as you get older and your height reduces and you become less physically active, your weight tends to increase. It follows that a reduction in height requires a reduction in weight to keep the BMI ratio on target. Does this mean that if one survives to be over a hundred years old and you follow this BMI policy – where reduced height means reduced weight – you would shrink to a size where tall people wouldn't be able to see you and trip over you? You would be walked on, your pet dog could eat you. You'll need a child's booster seat to drive the car – but your legs won't reach the pedals. It's OK if they get the driverless cars to work properly by then, but there's another worry in a pedestrian situation: will driverless car sensors see someone that small on the road and stop in time?

I've worked out that the free healthy area window sits somewhere between thirty and fifty. If you experience an accident or a mishap within that period of your life, the medical people then make you feel like you're just plain stupid.

This is usually achieved by a shaking of their head and some statement of obviousness. 'This could have been very serious. How did you possibly do this to yourself?'– as if you have some type of uncontrollable masochistic trait. Or the classic, 'Well, you won't be doing that again in a hurry, will you?' I wasn't in a hurry this time – it took me forty years to get the first one in.

Another favourite is, 'You're fortunate you're young enough to get over this quite quickly. If you were, say, twenty years older, it would have been a lot more serious.' These medical people just can't wait until you're older so they can do that 'Well, at your age' routine.

Either side of that thirty to fifty years' window, we're either too young or too old.

I have a close relative around my age who passed out while walking into her bedroom one morning, falling to the floor on her back. When she woke up looking at the ceiling, although she estimated she was only out for a few minutes, she fully realised what had just happened could be something very serious. She immediately sought a medical explanation and was in due course informed that the tests have not indicated any reason for her sudden unplanned, unconscious and horizontal state.

The doctor added that all the tests have indicated she could live to be one hundred. I thought that may well be the case, but only if she ensures she continues to pass out in selected, affable and safe places; avoiding situations like nearly to the top of a flight of stairs, or driving a car, or cooking and going bye-byes just as she turned the gas on but hadn't lit it yet.

She was duly informed – 'But at your stage in life you do need to take things a bit easier and enjoy life.'

I thought how much easier can you get? Walking around her single storey house, then suddenly lying on thickly carpeted floor at any non-selected moment? This also has the element of surprise about it too and that is surely a good thing for enjoying life?

In my early fifties I suffered a bout of influenza which just wouldn't go away – I gave this awful thing a home for the best part of two weeks. The major flu like symptoms had faded, but it left me with an unwell feeling including, an annoying headache and this prevented any worthwhile restful sleep for a number of days. I consulted with a GP who was around thirty-five years old, emphasising the sleeping issue, as I thought if I could get some decent sleep the body will catch up and beat this thing.

I was advised to take life a bit easier, slow down and maybe look at getting an easier job (I was in a managerial role at the time). But no assistance with the sleeping was forthcoming. The prescription was, take a few days off work and rest.

The health became worse, so I went back two days later and this time demanded something to clear this thing up and get some sleep.

I then received my first medical lecture on getting older. It was suggested that I be referred to a psychologist to help me understand the ageing process better; it would assist in improving my health and general outlook on life, by accepting the slowing down concept. I'm fifty-two, for God's sake. This sombre outlook gives me a life span of around fifty-five.

This was the first time I actually seriously and openly questioned some doctor's legal ability to practise – well, on humans anyway. I stormed out of that GP (more like shuffled out, given my energy state), and went down a block to another more experienced GP. It was quickly diagnosed as a bacterial infection, seemingly left over from the flu, and my body was being slowly poisoned. An antibiotic course and some sleeping pills and I was back on the road to normality in three days.

In my reflective moments now, I wonder if this is a general trait for young GPs who, as soon as they see a patient twenty years older than themselves, immediately write the patient off with the old age diagnosis. Everything you get wrong with you from then on is to be expected at your age.

The plan seems to be that the holistic medical profession and more can all get a bit of action out of this. This value-adding or upselling may include the psychologist, the dietitian, the nutritionist, the physiotherapist, the medical imaging industry, the pharmacist and a huge range of old age support services right up to the retirement home and the funeral industry on the end of the list.

A major part of the medical degree, I'm sure, includes training on the ability to quickly recognise an aged human and then tell them they are old as some sort of chargeable diagnosis.

I had a work colleague, Keith, about my age, who sought medical advice some ten years ago from a bulk-billing medical centre about what seemed to be chronic insomnia and what caused it, the effective treatments and community assistance currently available. The young doctor allocated to Keith's case quickly interrupted him during his reason for being there story, to reassure him that insomnia is a common and therefore natural occurrence for some people at his time of life and it should be expected.

The doctor quickly indicated he would prescribe a mild sedative to start with, when Keith jumped straight in with, 'Will you please listen. I am trying to explain to you I'm not here for myself. I'm after expert medical advice for my teenage grandson who lives with us, who walks around the house most of the night opening and closing doors, watching television and the like. He claims he just can't sleep, but I suspect illicit drugs may be involved. What can I do, as he won't go near a doctor?'

Still wanting to treat Keith, the doctor asked how he was sleeping.

'I'm not sleeping well at the moment because my grandson is walking around the bloody house all night. Before he started this, usually I slept very well.'

After eventually dispensing the appropriate advice to Keith for his grandson, the doctor concluded the consultation with, 'But at your age, Keith, you shouldn't worry too much. I can see you're rather tense now. Try to cut back on stressful situations. Would you be prepared to discuss the issue with a psychologist I can recommend?'

Keith was never known as a man of infinite tolerance, and I applauded his reported calm but pointed response to this doctor. 'It's very simple, doctor. Firstly, my stress level has just doubled since I came through your door because you won't listen. Secondly, if your medical profession, collectively, can just get my bloody zombie, android of a grandson to sleep properly, at proper times, I'll be fine. I don't need any psychologist, thank you.'

I attended a GP doctor to have an annual skin check-up for any of the nasties that attack and invade our protective layer from time to time. The medico was supposed to be something of an expert in the field and I hadn't consulted with him previously.

He was around the mid-thirty to forty age group, had a heavy Asian accent and was nowhere near as fluent in English as one would hope for an Australian doctor. I explained why I was there and he asked that I go behind the curtain and disrobe and he would be with me shortly. 'Please, you will take all clothes off. There is an examination stretcher there for you to sit on,' he directed.

I thought it was a bit strange – all the clothes? It's usually just the shirt and long trousers. Oh well, maybe he was more thorough than others I had attended.

Just as I had completely disrobed, his telephone rang and even in his bad English I picked up enough of the conversation to understand the meaning and become immediately alarmed.

He said to the caller, 'No, no, I cannot see any more patients today. I have to leave here by one o'clock and I've got to do this vasectomy which will take most of that time.'

My antenna went up straight away and locked on the panic channel. He had to do a vasectomy? That was why I disrobed completely? His command of English was poor. Had he got me mixed up with another patient? He didn't seem to comprehend what I was saying to him when I first came in. Bloody hell. I was out of there and was well on the way to getting dressed when he came behind the curtain.

He said, 'No, no, all clothes off, please.'

I said, 'No, no, all clothes back on and I'm out of here. I'm not your vasectomy patient – there's been a mix-up. I overheard your telephone conversation.'

He looked puzzled then explained that vasectomy operations were done in the procedures room, not here. If I wanted a vasectomy, I needed to make another appointment to discuss it. 'You said you want skin examination, now you also want vasectomy?' he questioned. He went on to explain he couldn't do a vasectomy then as he had to leave straight after he did the vasectomy for the next patient. 'Now, get clothes off again please and we start with skin examination.'

'Oh, you were talking about the next patient?' I said, rather sheepishly.

We did start and I kept a close watch on his every move and what implement he had in his hand when he got to inspect around and below the waistline.

His parting request was for me to make sure I booked in with reception on my way out for the next appointment to discuss the vasectomy.

I paid for that first visit and got out of there as quickly as I could. No new appointment necessary, thanks.

I have a great old mate in New Zealand who unfortunately suffered a fairly serious stroke some years back that affected the movement and control of his arms and hands. After a while into the recovery program, Bill discussed with me the recuperation plan he was on and noted that some of the exercisers were not all that encouraging for an impatient man as he was. He was happy that he had any number of pretty young therapist ladies attending to his every need and he was making reasonable progress. One exercise in particular was that of typing his name, address and other details that he should be able to recall readily, which apparently is a well known stroke treatment exercise.

He understood that the exercise was originally used years before the wide availability of computers and word processors and started on the mechanical typewriter. The typewriter key only produced the one letter on the page each time it was struck. Holding the key down for a long period still only produced the one letter. However, given that the computer will continuously reproduce the letter on the screen while ever the key is depressed, Bill ended up with seventeen pages of 'B', ten and a half pages of 'i' and somewhere around twenty pages of the letter 'l' before he could get his finger to release the particular keys.

Bill was not a computer savvy person, but has a fantastic sense of humour. Instead of the designed discernible reward for his effort, he was left with an outcome that annoyed him no end. As he said to me, 'I couldn't get the bloody thing to stop – it just kept on going and going and going and it seemed to get faster. I only wanted one of each letter.'

I have developed this persistent dripping nose that seems to happen every time I eat anything – doesn't seem to matter what it is. I've had all the allergy tests done with no definite results. My regular doctor has tried different remedies but to no avail as it still keeps dripping every time I eat. At times I feel like a little puppy dog with a permanently wet nose, which I thought in the canine world meant the dog was very healthy.

I haven't started scratching behind my ears with my hind legs yet or sniffing other people in embarrassing places, so I don't think there are any serious canine traits coming through at this stage. But, and I'm not sure if this is related, I have all of a sudden taken a particular and peculiar interest in noisy cars and motorbikes going past. I also look forward to the postman coming along each day, but I don't think that means anything.

I must be allergic to something – but the allergy tests can't find anything. I'm beginning to believe I'm allergic to myself. My doctor says that assumption is ridiculous but, as I pointed out (and he has no answer for this), we have tried everything and the only things that are still common that we haven't changed and have been in place all the time, is the air I breathe and the body I live in. I don't think we can do much about either. But as long as the wet nose continues, I should be healthy.

At least I haven't had the blanket cover diagnosis of, 'Well, at your age…' That is probably mainly due to the fact that this doctor's age is not far behind mine.

3

Tall Stories, Rumours & Old Yarns

Every country community has its own characters – the type of people who either make up and broadcast stories that become local folklore or the wags in the community who invented the stories about people, which in turn become attached to a particular local identity.

Where I grew up in a small town in the south-west of New South Wales around the fifties, we had a branch line rail service that delivered most of the goods or freight to the town and district. This cargo, which was usually just parcels, was picked up at the railway station by carriers and subsequently delivered to the business houses in the town or further afield to the surrounding farming community.

One such carrier was Ned Bourne, who also carried out other transport delivery services around the state. Ned seemed to have a never ending assortment of tall stories to relate. He had a dry humorous comment on most things but his stories of his own experiences were probably the most entertaining. Here are some of his claims to success over the years.

He once carted four and a half ton of loose ping-pong balls from Sydney to Melbourne on a flat tray truck without a rope or a net. He claimed the trick was all in the way you stacked them.

He also claimed that he once shifted a large Sydney-based pet shop, fittings and animals, to Brisbane in his largest steel-covered van in a non-stop trip. He was a bit overloaded so, to keep the weight down going up hills, he had rigged up a rope tied from the back door of the van, along the truck side, to the passenger door, and his offsider passenger would repeatedly flick the rope against the metal side of the van, frightening all the birds off their perches, therefore reducing the weight. Once over the hill, the rope flicking would stop and the birds would rest easy back on their perch.

The pet shop owner met Ned at the destination and when they opened the van, the owner couldn't understand why all his birds appeared exhausted and extremely traumatised, with little feathers still floating in the air, yet all the other non-flying animals were well rested. In response to his concern, Ned replied it was his experience that some breeds of birds don't travel very well in a northerly direction. Something to do with they think they're always flying uphill, and I can vouch for that – they sure don't like going uphill.

I'm not sure who to attach this one to as it seemed to be told by a few people. The teller of the story was in a conversation about long-livers and subsequently recalled that when he was walking through the town park one day, he saw a man who seemed to be in his mid-seventies, sitting on his own under a tree crying, sobbing so sadly. The passer-by thought the old man must be seriously injured or he had received some really bad news. Maybe a close relative had passed away – maybe even his wife. The storyteller thought he needed to try to console the old man, so he asked what the matter was and could he help him in any way.

The old man explained he was crying because his father had just chastised him severely, including giving him a hiding with the strap.

His father? How old must his father be, the Good Samaritan wondered to himself. This can't be right, he thought – he must have misheard – but he played along. 'Tell me,' he asked of the old man, 'Why did your father chastise you?'

Through the sobbing, the old man said, 'For throwing stones at Grandpa.'

Now that was a family of long-livers.

In another small country town where I worked and lived for five years in pre-internet days, social discussion topics in the pubs usually centred on what the local upper class was doing: who had just bought or sold what property, how the local footy team played last weekend, the latest gossip around the local romantic goings-on – who had just shacked up with who – the effect of the current weather conditions on the local farming community, and many more rather boring conversations.

A friend and I were discussing this end of the world stuff over a beer at the local bowling club one evening, bemoaning the fact that there never seemed to be any challenging conversation topics, no new ideas or business opportunities to discuss on the broader community front.

One such opportunity that seemed to be popular around Australia then was that of rearing rabbits for both their pelt and their meat. We decided that was something that would go well where we lived, given the rather isolated location. There always seemed to be small landholdings up for sale and available and plenty of rabbit fodder accessible from local farmers. Our interest increased in just how this industry operated – mainly just out of curiosity.

We discussed it a few times now and then and, as is the case in these stickybeak small towns, everyone wanted to know what your business was. The club barman knew what we were discussing and got into the conversation from time to time; it was obvious he had responded to other club patron's questions as to what we were talking about.

One prominent farmer sidled up to us at the bar one evening and interrupted our conversation on some other subject, to inform us that this rabbit farm business we were contemplating would not be welcome and assured us he spoke on behalf of all the local farmers. The main gist of his verbal serve was that if those rabbits got out, the buggers would spread like a plague. 'We farmers spend a lot of time and money getting rid of the bastards and we don't want someone here breeding any more of them.'

We then realised that our rabbit farm discussions had caused some major discontent in the local farming community. We were both elated that the club and pub talk had now turned to this subject and we just accepted the negative talk and played along, saying it was just in the very early stages. There was no definite proposal at this point.

I even received phone calls from the farming community complaining about the proposal. On one occasion, I was informed that the caller would bring pressure to bear on the council planning management to ensure the project didn't go ahead. Another farmer threatened to report our proposal to the local Pastures Protection Board (I think it's now the Rural Lands Protection Board).

When we decided enough was enough, we told those who wanted to listen that it all started as harmful gossip from people overhearing a private conversation that had nothing to do with them and making it their business to become the knowledgeable experts on the subject. We did not have a proposal for a rabbit farm.

We should have known better, as the response was that the reasons the rabbit farm was not going ahead was that we had failed to get council planning permission and that caused our financial backers to pull out. That should teach us to think again about introducing any such change – things were just right the way they were.

For quite a while afterwards, I thought the matter had blown over, I would often get the odd ribbing like, 'How's that rabbit farm going eh? You sure got stopped there, didn't you?'

There was a quote that I can't identify the original author of, that went something like this: 'One of the good things about living in a small town is that when you don't know what you're doing, someone else surely does.'

In a different small town I lived in for over twenty years, there were always stories invented to either embarrass people or make fun of their circumstances, or start a rumour just to see how far it would go. One in particular I recall was started by a person who had little respect for the long term local Catholic church parish priest, a Father Harrison. He started a very convincing rumour around the pubs on a Monday evening that Father Harrison had suffered a heart attack that morning and had died at the presbytery. He enhanced the story by saying it had been arranged with the funeral directors to keep the body there for a day or two for anyone wanting to pay their respects, given that he would be buried in his original home town in another part of the state.

I heard of a few people who went to the presbytery on Tuesday morning to pay their respects only to be met by the said priest opening the door. A few of the visitors would have experienced wobbly legs, I dare say.

One classic story of the 'lying in state viewing' was about two old ladies, both devoted churchgoers, neither in the best of health and evidently keen to get as many heavenly credits as they could muster. They were met at the front door by the housekeeper and in a solemn tone said they were there to visit with Father Harrison and pay their respects. The housekeeper, apparently thinking it was just a visit from parishioners, ushered them into a front sitting room and asked them to wait there. While they were waiting, their conversation included an update on each other's failing health, but more importantly they decided they should pray for the recently departed priest and they burst into sincere and audible prayer.

By that time in the day, the priest had become aware of the rumour but there was no way to really stop it completely (there were no social media in those days) and he was not in a good mood. He walked to the sitting room door facing the back of the ladies' chairs just as they had mentioned his name in their prayer.

This priest had a very distinctive and loud voice. He evidently said something like, 'Hello, ladies. Thank you for the prayers and it's good to see you're both joining me here today.'

I understood their reaction to Father Harrison's resurrection or heavenly invitation was a bit more than just surprised.

This version of their solemn visitation was related by the husband of one of the ladies. He had brought home the original news of the passing of the priest from the pub and now he was looking for the instigator, because he was subject to a fair bit of hell (no heaven on offer) at home as a result.

I was told of a story that happened back in the days of the first home soda fountains where you could fill the rather large bottle with whatever

'GOOD TO SEE YOU LADIES ARE JOINING ME TODAY'

still beverage you wanted, pressurise it with a small CO_2 gas cylinder attachment and shoot the beverage through the dispenser nozzle over a reasonable distance.

This story centres on a house party where a pet cockatoo in its cage on the back veranda was seemingly objecting to the party invitees and kept screeching very loudly, in turn upsetting the partygoers.

Two partygoers who the bird was annoying more so than the rest emptied the water out of the soda fountain bottle and part refilled it with a strong water and gin mix, and recharged the fountain.

They sat next to the cocky's cage and every time the bird opened its beak to squawk, they would shoot the liquid straight into its mouth.

After a few shots, the desired effect was achieved – cocky was asleep on the bottom of the cage. The storyteller didn't relate how long cocky was out to it, but I'm sure if it woke up as cantankerous as humans do with a hangover, they probably had to administer the keep-quiet elixir again.

In the days before electronic poker machines, such gambling devices had a purely mechanical mechanism with no power connection at all and a case made of heavy cast steel to prevent easy opening and stealing of the coins within. The machines were only found in licensed clubs.

Now and then, some of the older-type machines would tend to stick and not pay out the correct amount of coins on a win. One of the tried and true methods to fix the short pay was to lift the front of the machine up a few inches and drop it back down on its base. This practice was frowned on by club management everywhere.

I witnessed this behaviour from a short in stature man who was well inebriated, playing such a poker machine in a country-based club, and the rewards for his effort were not pleasing him. So in an attempt to show the machine that he was boss and that he wanted some of his money back, he employed the pick-up-and-drop practice.

The club steward on duty instructed him to cease or he would be asked to leave the premises – he would be thrown out and possibly his membership cancelled.

Telling the steward to go away, he continued, but to no avail. He was still losing money.

In his scrambled brain, he must have thought a higher pick up and drop was required and he lifted the heavy machine in a cuddle hold much higher than before only to find that, with the combination of his diminished reflexes, his short stature and his wobbly boot state, the machine took over and the momentum made him back-pedal some distance before falling backwards over a table with the machine still on his chest. He screamed for assistance, as he knew even in his demented state that if he dropped and broke the machine, he would have to pay for it.

The steward ambled down to assist him, placed the machine back on the stand and duly threw him out.

In my country town back in the seventies, a persistent have-a-chat bloke named Frank had a well-known habit of cadging a ride home from the local pub when he had more than enough to drink and then wouldn't get out of your car once at home – he kept wanting to talk pure rubbish. No matter how much you insulted him, nothing got rid of him until he had to go to the toilet.

Trying to do a favour, I fell for doing this a few times, making Frank pre-promise that he would get out of the car as soon as I got him home meant nothing. One night, I got so frustrated with him not getting out at his house that I drove off with him still in the passenger seat.

'Where are you going?' he asked with surprise.

I said, 'I just told you seven times, I have to go home, so that's where I'm going. You can walk back to your house from there when you're ready.'

He pleaded that I couldn't do that to him – he was too drunk to walk that far. So I pulled up at the end of his block and gave him the option that he got out here and now, or he could walk from my house, which would have been around seven town blocks away, uphill and across a railway line. The talking continued and he wouldn't get out so

I drove to my house, parked in front and left him in the vehicle, much to his displeasure. I went inside. I had a look about fifteen minutes later and he was gone.

The local pub we had just come from was much closer than his house, and I was informed later that week that Frank staggered there and bludged another ride home after telling all how big of a bastard I was. The next Good Samaritan offered the ride just to get rid of him out of the pub but he experienced the same problem – Frank wouldn't stop talking and wouldn't get out, so the driver drove off taking Frank back to the pub he started from. Return to sender. The driver got out and went back into the pub. Frank followed, pleading for the ride home but with no success. The Return to Sender man told Frank he was an idiot, he had the chance but blew it – never again.

His next target that night was a young man with a ute who was just on his way home. The publican warned him about Frank's have-a-chat habit and the ute driver said it was OK as he would have to get in the back of the ute anyway, because he had some equipment in the front seat and he had no intention of shifting it.

Into the back our ride bludger got and the ute driver told Frank he had three minutes to get out when they get to his house; if he didn't, he would end up travelling to the driver's farm some twenty kilometres away – all the way in the back of the ute. They arrived at Frank's house. Frank staggered and half fell out of the back, and as soon as the driver saw Frank in the rear-view mirror walking towards the driver's door, obviously to start the habitual nonsensical chatting, he sped off, showering him with stones from the roadway.

Frank had a busy and adventurous night. My estimate was that it took him over three hours to eventually get home and inside his house from the pub, which should normally be a journey of some ten minutes maximum by car.

Frank didn't frequent that particular pub for a while after this experience – it must have been three months before he turned up there again. But I have to give him credit that, despite the rumours, the grog hadn't completely stuffed his brain – well, not the memory anyway – for the next time I saw him in that pub, he went around asking everyone else for a lift home except the 'Return to Sender' man and me. Lesson well learned, I think. I think the young man with the ute was also completely out of any future consideration for Frank.

Here is another one from the annals of drinking places. This one suggested to me from one who tried it.

Hubby comes home very late one night from the pub. He takes five minutes to get the key in the lock, then staggers, near falls in the front door. He then tries to sneak quietly down the dark hallway when the light goes on at the end and there is the wife with a very sour look on the face, arms folded and a cold stare aimed at her inebriated hubby.

He recognises immediately without a word being spoken that this look demands an answer as to why he is so drunk and so late. Hubby is no fool – even in his state, he can still think on his feet. Remembering what one of his mates told him some time ago on the subject of good excuses, he offers the following response. 'I'm sorry I'm late, dear. I was just about to leave the pub a few hours ago, when it was announced there was to be a competition there tonight to see who had the loveliest and most understanding wife, so I had to stay to nominate you. And I got you into the final. I'll bet you're pleased about that.'

My informant reported that it didn't work.

My friend Harold lived in an upmarket Sydney suburb surrounded by very conservative neighbours – the type who frown on any noise after seven o'clock at night.

In his job, Harold entertained clients regularly and occasionally late into the night, causing him to arrive home the worse for wear, alcoholically speaking, at times. This night was one such night. His wife was getting very tired of his late homecomings, so to teach him a lesson she had the front and back door locks changed that day.

Around ten o'clock, Harold approaches the front door to find his key doesn't work and then tries the back door with the same results. Just then the wife calls out from the upstairs window informing Harold he can sleep somewhere else tonight – she has had the locks changed and has locked him out.

Being a resourceful, well organised, quiet and unflappable person, Harold, without saying a word back, walks a short distance from the back door to his workshop shed, runs out an extension cord and plugs his power saw in. He then switches on the saw and begins sawing an entry opening into his back door – a space big enough for him to get in is the plan for this DIY project.

This sets the wife off screaming hysterically as she hurries downstairs in a frantic effort to stop him, but to no avail. She calls the police, every neighbourhood dog starts barking or howling, close neighbours also call the police, reporting a power saw massacre madman on the rampage. Several police turn up in multiple cars, sirens wailing, arriving just in time to see Harold completing his late night handyman job of how to create a new entry space.

After proving to the police he is the homeowner and currently lives there, he suggests he could do what he wants to his own back door – including sawing it up into little pieces if he wants to.

The police have to agree that the only issue here may be one of disturbing the peace, but no one except his wife has complained, and it's thought she may have been a contributing factor anyway.

No domestic violence is reported – how could there be, because Harold was locked out and when he did get in, the extension cord was only long enough to do the door job. He would have had to throw the thing to do any more damage with it inside, unless he took the time to consistently replug it as he moved through the house – hardly the style of a person dedicated to inflict instant damage. Also, he was hardly thought to be sneaking up on his wife.

The police leave the premises and all the inquisitive neighbours go back to bed.

So, after temporary door repairs, Harold slept in his own bed that night and his wife caught a cab to her mother's place for the night.

And, I think next day, the locksmith, as well as the door installation people, got another job out of it.

4

For Charitable and Community Purposes

Working for charitable purposes, or to assist the community generally, is in itself rewarding to most people and I have enjoyed the small bit I have been involved with from time to time.

In my small home town in my early twenties, I was dobbed in as president of a festival queen fund-raising committee aimed at accumulating monies for a new swimming pool complex in the town. The concept was that two queens were nominated and the winner was determined by the most funds raised by their supporting committees over the designated time frame.

We conducted the usual events – raffles, dances and the like – and we also came up with some new ones now and again. None of us really knew how they would turn out, but we tried anyway.

One of the new events was a car gymkhana conducted on the basic format of an equine gymkhana including flag races, timed obstacle courses, a timed hill climb and a few more new automobile-related competitions.

The event was conducted on private property and that caused some issues with insurance, but we eventually got that covered off. Trying to do the right thing, we involved the local police and considered their advice on the running of the event. One of their stipulations was that no alcohol was to be served on site and no drivers under the influence of alcohol would be allowed to compete. Being on private property, the police had little power in the vehicle usage area. However, we needed to do the right thing by them and we tried hard to meet their requests.

We invited them to visit the site at any time during the event and they did show up about halfway through the day and towards the conclusion.

The halfway inspection was satisfactory. However, the last one did cause some problems. I was talking to the sergeant at the bottom of the area we used as a hill climb, when suddenly his eyes became wider as he stared over my shoulder then pulled me back a few paces with him. I turned round just in time to see a car coming towards us – the wrong way and off track – down the hill climb course, with three young men riding on the bonnet. All competition had ceased and these idiots were just skylarking.

Through his drunken vision and his bonnet passengers' bodies, the driver noticed the police and jammed on the brakes, and the three people lost their grip and slid ever so gracefully off the bonnet, coming to a stop on the ground at the sergeant's feet. They finished up in the middle of a rocky outcrop, which would have hurt a lot, but there were no immediate complaints. They were obviously well intoxicated from the pub, which didn't help our cause one bit.

The sergeant looked at me and said something like he thought the event should be like these three, and come to an appropriate and abrupt stop right now. He then tore strips off the driver and the drunks from the bonnet.

We closed up not long after. The local public enthusiasm was there to run another car gymkhana, but none of us on the committee were game to go to the police with the suggestion.

Country dances were always popular and we ran a few with different levels of success. We had a few small villages around the local shire and they were always well attended by the village folk, but we had to get the people from larger towns to travel there as the population in the villages would not make it worthwhile after you paid for a band, insurance and hall rent. We tried one in the furthest village from our town in that shire with the hope we might get some patronage from a neighbouring larger community. To support the dance fund raising, we decided to conducted a chocolate wheel raffle as well.

For the benefit of the uninformed, chocolate wheels are where people purchase numbered tickets and the organiser spins a wheel with numbers matching those on the tickets. Once the wheel stops on a specific number, the person holding that numbered ticket wins a prize. Legally, chocolate wheels were, and are now, only to be used for fund raising by registered charities, which we were. They are, as the name suggests, originally designed to raffle off boxes of chocolates, food hamper prizes and the like, but we couldn't see that gaining much attention from the crowd.

Frozen chooks were always a good prize, but to keep them frozen in such a situation was not easy. We had only around six in eskies loaded with ice and the plan was that any winners from the village could take them straight home to their fridge.

However, the three men running the wheel thought the chooks were not doing the job and the feeling of the crowd was right to start our Plan B: raffling money – a cash envelope. This is apparently legal in some states now but not then. You needed a special gambling permit which we didn't have.

They were doing great and had gathered a great crowd and making good money for us. I left them to it and went back to the dance.

After a while, one of the wheel operators came into the hall to tell me a policeman was out there and had closed the wheel down and wanted to talk to the person in charge – it appeared we needed to produce the gambling licence to raffle the money.

We thought originally we were fairly safe as there was no police station in this village. This policeman was stationed at a nearby village, but covered this area – and covered it very well that night.

I approached the policeman and the ensuing discussion indicated he had the right to close the money wheel down. I asked if we could raffle frozen chooks – and yes, that was no problem. We opened the wheel again, raffling chooks – the whole remaining four.

After a while, when we thought we were all clear, one of our wheel agents would deliver the chook to the winner in the crowd and subsequently offer cash equal to the money we were providing during the money wheel, to buy the chooks back from the winner. We would then raffle it again. It could be said we were again raffling money.

At one stage, there was hardly anyone in the hall and no one on the dance floor. Even the band members took a long break and came out to see what was happening.

It didn't seem to matter to the patrons, but the frozen chooks were no longer frozen. They were now limp chooks.

The policeman came up to me again – we thought he had left the village but he had been watching from the shadows and indicated to me that he knew what we were doing and he couldn't stop us. But he warned that if any antisocial behaviour developed out of this gambling activity he would come down on us like a ton of bricks for something – didn't matter what, he would think of something.

He added, 'Unofficially, good luck with the fund raising but be aware there are some real wowsers in this village and when they complain about the gambling, my report will show I closed you up once. You'll be on your own then.'

There were only around six chooks to start with and the biggest problem was that most of the local women who won a chook kept the bloody thing for Sunday lunch. We had one left we could use – it was that defrosted you could put your fingers through to touch near its backbone. We thought we were safe with this one; no one would want to keep it for Sunday lunch. But one lady winner of this last disgusting-looking limp fowl would not part with it and that closed the wheel activity down.

We had to announce to the crowd it was all over as we had run out of chooks.

One local man said to me that he had one in the freezer at home that he could go and get. How much would we give him for it so we could keep going? He wanted far too much.

Another local man; a husband of one of the earlier lady winners who had taken her winnings home to the freezer and returned, asked me quietly if he went home and stole the chook the wife won earlier out of the freezer, would we buy that? Again, the price was way too high and the crowd was thinning, so we closed it up.

The band was happy – they had someone to dance to their music. Wives and girlfriends were happy as the menfolk were back to dance with them. We committee members were happy – we made more money than we had imagined for the cause.

Most Australians are aware of the Tamworth Country Music Festival and the associated Australasian Country Music Awards that began in the early 1970s. This story came to me from a mate in Tamworth. John used to assist in the many community-based functions that made the event so successful over the years.

In 2004, heavy rain in the catchment caused a flash flood in the Peel River, which runs through the city centre of Tamworth. Thousands of festival campers were woken very early on Saturday morning by the SES and told to evacuate. The word was through that flooding on the Cockburn River was about to hit the Peel River and just hours later the sports ground where they were camped would be covered in up to a metre of water.

One camper, who, it turned out, had a very heavy drinking session on the Friday night, returned to the campsite and had need to use the portable toilets provided. He locked himself in and unfortunately passed out cold on the seat. In his self-administered unconscious state, he failed to respond to the evacuation orders from the SES, which apparently included banging on all the toilet doors asking if anyone was in there and delivering the evacuation orders. There was also apparently no time available for much of the campers' facilities, including the portable toilets, to be moved to higher ground. Getting the people and their personal belonging out was of course the top priority.

Consequently, when the flood waters rose to a sufficient level, he went floating away (probably not so graciously), bobbing along and eventually heading down the Peel River.

John reported that the good ship *Portaloo* eventually got completely

snagged on some debris somewhere downstream a few hours later and thankfully in an upright position. It rested against a piece of timber near the river bank so the door couldn't be opened from inside. Despite his hectic voyage, the intrepid lone sailor was duly rescued by the SES after making himself hoarse from hours of yelling out for help. He was not in the best of condition when rescued; bruised, battered, smelly but fairly sober now. Reportedly, when rescued and he stepped out on to dry land, he said, 'I thought at first it was a drunken nightmare – you know, when you yell out and no one hears you, when you have a fit of the horrors – but then I thought, no, it's too real, I must have died and on my way to hell in a bloody portaloo.'

Another fund-raising effort for a community project in the late sixties, again as part of a queen competition, was a carnival night designed to raise funds through the traditional sideshow stands – knock-'em-downs, lucky envelopes, raffles, kids' pony rides and so on.

Two of us on the committee got the idea to set up a kissing booth – copying off the American movies we used to see in those days. We convinced around five young ladies to supply the smooches but with their strict condition there must be a capable, responsible bodyguard there to look after them at all times – someone physically capable who could get any troublemakers to move along. We agreed.

I thought who better than one of our committee members, a good friend of our queen candidate, a big bloke, well respected by other likely clients – perfect. I had a talk to him and explained what we wanted and I was assured it would be OK – he would do it.

We set up the stand just in time. The girls turned up but no bodyguard. He arrived late and rather the worse for wear. After our initial conversation earlier in the day, he had got thinking about it and got a bit nervous, so he had a few beers to settle down – the few turned into a few more and he was extremely relaxed when he reported for duty. Relaxed to the point of being rather amorous. He started trying to kiss all the girls for free – they left en masse and headed for the safety of the mingling crowd.

And that was the end of our fund-raising trump card. You could say our bodyguard actually tried to steal the bodies he was supposed to be guarding.

5

Work Is Not All Work

I don't think it matters what job you do in Australia, there is always an amusing happening at some stage if people can only see it. Such happenings may not be side-splittingly funny but they are usually vastly different enough from the everyday humdrum of the job to create at least a good chuckle.

In my fifty-odd working years, I have experienced quite a few entertaining instances and space here does not permit a great number to be retold at this time. I have also had some reported to me that could have resulted in serious accidents. However, given that no one was life-threateningly harmed, I see a humorous side to the outcomes.

Most of my working life has been spent either directly employed in the rural electricity supply industry or in support organisations, including my own consultancy business.

In about the early 1970s, a small group of us were working on a substation at a rural property with just a shearing shed connected to the supply. I had a sudden call of nature and thankfully there was an old pit toilet there I could make use of.

After clearing the majority of bugs and cobwebs away, I was relieved to take up the desired position on the seat. Such was this relief that I failed to initially notice a large redback spider crawl up my overalls until I felt it arrive on my bare upper leg. This species was common there, especially inside switchboard panels, where the larger more aggressive female would come straight at you when they were disturbed. I had many run across my hands and arms in such situations but this was a new experience.

This one was a large female and it moved quickly across the top of my leg to the inside leg, then stopped and appeared to be teetering on entering the scrotum area. What could I do? I couldn't get a clean whack at it. If I missed, it might attack me. If I didn't, it might go even further into my private property. The latter occurred and I couldn't get any sort of hit at it or flick it off.

I then felt great trepidation and apprehension as it decided my scrotum area was the place to be. The fear increased as it continued on its journey of discovery.

Unless you have experienced it first hand, I don't think anyone can understand the level of uncertainty of this situation. You're not game to finish off what you started to do in case that causes it to react aggressively; you can't quite work out where it is or where it's going. Would it get tangled in the pubics? Or would it decide to set up camp down there and start a web? I couldn't go through life with a colony of redbacks in my crutch.

Thankfully, it eventually lost interest, came up the other leg and quickly moved on out the other side and onto the seat. I still had nothing suitable to swat it with. I was just thankful for its departure. I carefully flicked it off the seat and resumed my composure, now with a wide-ranging eagle eye for any of its followers.

I then thought, where did it come from? Did it come out of the overalls dangling around my lower legs, or did it crawl up the outside of my clothing? I wasn't sure. However, on standing back up, I did make a thorough search of the clothing I was about to put back on.

When I related my story on my return to the worksite, there was absolutely no sympathy at all – just raucous laughter.

Another wildlife story came back from a workmate of mine sent out to a farm to replace an aerial electricity service cable to the farmer's house. He was on a ladder leaning against the house connecting that end of the cable and the farmer was standing nearby chatting.

Suddenly the farmer spied a brown snake coming out from under the adjacent rainwater tank stand and yelled at my mate not to move as there was a brown snake at the foot of his ladder. 'I'll get my shotgun – I'll get the bastard.' And he reached into a garden shed nearby and retrieved the gun.

My mate said, 'There's a what where? You'll get what? Where is it? Oh shit.' He looked down to see the snake starting to wind its way up the ladder stiles towards his baggy-legged shorts and he scrambled onto the flat roof of the house as the farmer let go with both barrels and reloaded.

Being keen to finish the job, the farmer got a bit carried away and another two barrels went off and the snake was done for. He was momentarily elated until he looked up to notice his old but full rainwater tank was now a picturesque fountain jetting water out of the many, many holes in the side just above the base, thanks to the many, many stray shot pellets from the shotgun cartridges.

My mate still had his face down on the roof.

The farmer yelled to him to get down quick and help him shove some twigs or something in the holes to stop the flow. 'I've shot me bloody tank.'

There was definitely no chance of my mate coming down until he was sure the shooting had stopped and the snake was dead. Last time he looked, it was still moving around the ladder base.

The farmer assured him the snake was dead and encouraged him again, this time with success, to help with plugging the tank holes. Any close twigs were part of a beautifully flowering well-manicured shrub – a real showpiece – but they had to be used.

The farmer's wife had heard the commotion from around the other side of the garden and arrived in time to see her beautiful plant being destroyed, water shooting out of her kitchen rainwater tank like a Roman fountain, and a bloodied heap of scaly stuff that was few minutes ago a big brown snake adjacent to her back door.

They saved a bit of water, but not the plant, and I think that marriage might have been on a rather shaky foundation for a while as well.

A new ladder was required, but how do you explain in a replacement requisition, to any level of satisfaction, that your ladder damage was the result of it being shot by four rounds from a twelve-gauge shotgun?

I was imagining this was something the farmer could boast about on the next shooting trip with his mates. 'Once, with just four shots, I killed a big brown snake, a rainwater tank and an extension ladder, took ten years off the life of an overhead line worker and about ten years of past good behaviour and accumulated brownie points off my marriage. Now beat that.'

Probably one of the most subtle practical jokes I've seen played on anyone in a workplace was at an office where I worked in the early nineties. To set the background, a newly employed young accountant (let's call him Don) had just purchased what he thought was the best motorbike in the touring class category available on the Australian market. It was his first new motorbike and it cost him heaps.

The only other motorbike enthusiast in the building was a section manager in the technical department and he had been into upmarket touring motorbikes for some years (let's call him John). However, unlike Don, he remained very quiet about his interest.

John was constantly annoyed with Don's snide remarks about how his brand was better and more reliable than John's choice and what outstanding experiences Don had the weekend before on the open road on his machine. Being 'one with the wind' stuff.

Don used to park his bike in a laneway between our two buildings. where it was effectively under the cover of a second-floor building bridge. In this position, it could be seen by office staff on that end of both buildings and more especially by John, who would see it from his work station on the second floor. John parked his bike with all the other traffic in the car park.

When he went to his wonderful machine one lunchtime, shock and horror as Don noticed there was a very small pool of motor oil on the ground just under the transmission. From his vantage point, John noticed the concerned antics of Don as he felt all over the bike to determine where exactly the oil had emanated from and seemingly without success.

Given that John was much more experienced in motorbikes, Don immediately consulted with him as to what could be the cause of this oil leak. John explained he didn't know anything about that brand of bike but, if it was him, he would have it straight back to the dealer as quickly as he could. Don agreed, and back to the dealer that afternoon he went.

Don reported back to John that the dealer found nothing wrong and Don said he was convinced there was nothing amiss with his wonderful machine. He was satisfied it was just one of those rare unexplained things you sometimes get with new top-class machines.

A few days later, John again copped a lecture on how great the Don bike was and the rather strong suggestion that John should really consider switching to his brand. John indicated that he was fine with his current machine, thanks.

Then again a few days later, another pool of oil appeared under Don's bike. So back to the dealer again and this time Don was ropeable. But apparently no immediate satisfaction from the dealer, who sent the problem to the manufacturer overseas. Don was informed it might take weeks to get a response.

Don once again brought his worry to John, who, in well demonstrated sympathy, suggested that it might not be a good idea to ride the bike on a long trip – you never know, you might get stuck out there on the road and especially late afternoon or at night, you didn't know who would come along. Someone with a ute and a few hefty blokes could load it up and steal it after leaving you broken in the gutter. He pointed out that Don alone should realise the money that bike would bring on the black market.

After a bit of consideration, Don indicated John was right. He hadn't thought of that. He decided he would just keep it for riding to work – that should be OK until he heard back from the manufacturer. John agreed that although the bike was built for the open road, you wouldn't want to wreck it completely until you found out what the problem really was.

The oil leak appeared a few more times and Don was nearly driven mad by that time as the manufacturer's response to the dealer suggested that the owner might be interfering with the bike and they threatened it would void the warranty.

Eventually Don found other employment in a neighbouring town, so John left his oil can at home from then on.

While we're in the area of office-located workers, a Sydney-based organisation had just picked up a large new client and it was imperative they do everything possible to please them on this initial order as it was to be the trial for any future business.

However, it became apparent that there might be a delivery problem looming in getting the goods to the new client on the time required and the general manager intervened to ensure that any delivery blockages would be eliminated.

The GM came from the company's head office in Hong Kong, very experienced in how the company worked but not very fluent in the English language in either the spoken or written word. He worked hard to ensure the goods would be with the client on the designated time, but alas, due to external reasons beyond the GM's control, delivery turned up a day late. The GM was furious and he immediately wrote an email apologising to the new client hoping to make amends and keep their business.

The email started with the usual heartfelt apology and the fact that the delay was beyond their control but finished with, 'I sincerely apologise for any incontinence that may have been experienced.' (Incontinence is just above inconvenience on Microsoft Office's spelling prompt.)

The client's manager twigged to the misspelling and responded that the goods did arrive intact as per the order. He thanked the GM for his concern for their health and yes, the day late delivery had given them the shits for a while. But he noted that any sign of incontinence passed fairly quickly.

There are always wags in the workplace and some do cause discomfort to others occasionally. One that always springs to mind is when a workshop supervisor was pushing a claim that he had developed anosmia – lost his sense of smell. I'm not sure who the claim was being aimed at but it was widely suspected in the workplace that there was some intent to gain financially from this condition.

Sympathy from his workmates was not apparent and, to test this claim out, his staff would enter his very small office on some false reason and deliver the best, silent as possible, fart that they could muster just to test out the claim and observe the result – whether he flinched, gasped for air or displayed any other normal signs of unsatisfactory air quality.

This experimental assessment was particularly popular on mornings after a night on the grog or in the late afternoons after a heavy curry lunch. I believe this non-medical testing regime was very effective when several testers entered the office on a cold winter's day when the office heater was on full blast.

Limited success was reported by some in that although no capitulation was ever indicated, there did seem to be excess watering of the eyes on occasions. The fact that at times the supervisor suddenly remembered he had to be somewhere else and leave the office was also claimed as a successful trial by some testers.

I'm not certain how it all panned out in the end. I think the testers got tired of their role, especially with the multiple tester scenario where they just couldn't stand the aroma of the fellow tester.

A container used as a worksite office was lifted into place and a young man obviously not trained in the crane chaser skills (or common sense), clambered on top of the load to unhook the crane hook. After he unhooked the load, instead of descending the ladder, he used to get up there, he directed the crane operator to lower the hook to the ground with the crane rope close to the edge of the container office they had just lifted into place. The crane operator had no idea what this was for, but he complied.

Then, much to the surprise of all others on the site, especially the crane operator, this idiot (there are much stronger words that could be used) jumped onto the crane rope and slid down to the ground like a trapeze artist or Tarzan on a vine.

What this clown didn't realise was that the steel rope of a crane that has been used for a while has small bits of wire sticking out all over it. The more used the rope, the more bits break and protrude.

The screams from the descending idiot was not unexpected by anyone knowledgeable in cranes and/or wire ropes, but it seemed to have been very unexpected by the Tarzanian worker. He was rushed to emergency with many lacerations and suspected steel bits in his legs, testicles, chest and arms. At least he had robust gloves on and his hands were safe.

I can imagine the admitting triage nurse saying, 'He did what? You have to be joking. Now, come on, what really happened? I can't put that in an official report. My boss will think I've been sampling the contents of the drug cabinet.'

The following story was reported at an industry meeting I attended, in a manner as serious as that in which it happened.

As I understood it, at a large bulk grain storage facility, the outgoing road delivery dispatch system consisted of empty, open-top trucks driving onto a weighbridge and stopping at the red light and being automatically weighed. Then, when instructed, the driver initiated the required amount of grain to be dumped into his truck from the silo hopper above. The weight was taken again and the system then recorded the amount to be charged to the particular client that delivery was destined for. Then a green light was shown and the driver departed the weighbridge on the way to the client.

The method to trigger the grain dumping was previously designed as a touch-screen panel within reach from where the truck driver stopped on the weighbridge. However, this proved impracticable due to different truck cabin heights and also extensive grain dust issues in the panel. Consequently, it was replaced with a simple, old-fashioned cord pull adjacent to the driver's door and long enough to be suitable for all cabin heights. One tug on the cord activated the electronic devise somewhere out of the dust, which delivered a designated amount of grain directly into the load area of the truck.

This reported incident occurred when the driver pulled the cord and the load of grain dropped as expected filling the truck. The driver, just as he was about to pull away, noticed something on the ground that took his attention, so he climbed out of his cabin to investigate. On resuming his cabin position, without noticing, he closed the cord pull in the cabin door.

Consequently, as he pulled away, another load full of grain that he didn't want dropped on his truck – not in it, but on it. He instinctively panicked and tried to get out of there pulling away again and another load of grain dumped on him. By this time, someone adjacent who could see what was happening and stopped the continuation of the raining of grain.

The system was apparently rejigged to prevent any future occurrence of this episode.

The following story comes to me from a coal mine where the mine management directed a large excavator to a position on a new area of the site they were planning to open up in the near future. The excavator was required to confirm the depth of the overburden by excavating the topsoil until he struck the expected top of the coal deposit. The coal deposit was found at around four metres as expected and the overburden spoil was left alongside the excavation. The excavator left the site.

A few days later, mine management sent one of their smaller dump trucks to the site to haul the spoil away, indicating to the driver that an overhead loader would be at the site shortly after him to carry out the loading.

This whole project had been held up due to excessive recent rain at the mine and the surrounding area, but all systems were now right to go.

The dump truck driver arrived at site and looked to park in a position that would be easy for the loader operator and for him. There were large puddles everywhere as a result of the recent prolonged heavy rain so it didn't matter much where he parked, as he wouldn't be getting out of the truck anyway to get wet feet, so in the middle of that puddle would be the best, he thought – close to the pile of overburden – and he drove towards it.

He actually drove straight into the four-metre-deep and five-metre-wide excavation that had filled to the top with the recent rain and on the surface looked like any other puddle. The dump truck went straight down nose first and he escaped through the hatch in the cabin roof and swam to the edge of the excavation to safety as the truck gurgled its way to rest on the bottom with its tail sticking out.

I understand that at the subsequent enquiry the dump truck driver had no answer for this question: 'Although there were several large puddles of rainwater around everywhere, and this filled up excavation looked like any one of the other puddles on the surface, where did you think that hill of soil came from that you were sent there to cart away? Would you not expect there might be a correspondingly sized hole in the ground somewhere very adjacent to that hill?'

Wet feet were not the only concern the driver had.

6

The Proper and Effective Use of Fireworks

A 'double-bunger' was a firework or cracker that made an extra loud noise and, for only about three inches long and a bit over half an inch thick, it had an accompanying powerful blast.

When crackers were legal for people – even kids – to purchase over the counter in most states, they were usually plentiful in all types of shops around the period leading up to what was known as Cracker Night on the long weekend in June. The official reason was to celebrate the Queen's birthday, but all kids knew it was opportunity to make a lot of noise and create some dazzling colourful displays. In country towns, Cracker Night was usually accompanied by a good-sized bonfire that the kids would have taken weeks to assemble.

The last Cracker Night in New South Wales to my memory was in 1986.

However, crackers being available for some time leading up to the official date caused some more unofficial uses of this popular urban explosive. Blowing up the mailboxes of the neighbours that kids didn't like was considered one accepted use.

Some kids became fairly skilled at estimating how much blast was required to demolish different types of mailboxes. An older type wooden one would usually take six or eight double-bungers held together with a rubber band to blow the lid off; and the skill was in twisting the wicks together at an equal distance from the bungers so to ensure all exploded at the same instant. A modern metal type could take up to ten well synchronised charges to make any impression, and then at times you would need to revisit the target a few times before satisfaction was achieved.

Not all kids in the neighbourhood hated the same neighbours, so if one successfully targeted neighbour was considered to be a good neighbour by another group of kids, the payback retaliation started and the unintended consequence was that the unfortunate postman had no mailbox to deliver to, so he had to deliver to the front door.

If the bunger charge was put into a mailbox with letters left in the box, the letters usually became confetti very quickly.

Another more serious bunger attack was where one or more was covertly slipped into the rear muffler outlet of a parked car. When the muffler got hot enough travelling along, the bunger was supposed to explode. I don't recall any reports of damage caused to the muffler but the explosion must have been quite worrying to the driver.

I heard a story about a young man of just legal drinking age was drunk and misbehaving in a country town pub, making an absolute nuisance of himself for what I understood was his first pub night out. The older regular patrons got tired of his stupid antics and the publican eventually threw him out.

He apparently gathered himself and returned to the pub an hour or so later with a packet of bungers which he lit and then threw in each bar door as he run past. Some of the older but agile drinkers chased and caught him, brought him back inside the bar, sat him in a chair next to them and placed what bungers he had left in a bundle in his lap right on top of what could be considered his most valuable bodily possessions at that age and told him if he moved they would light the bungers. To heighten the torment, periodically someone would flick a cigarette lighter near the bundle.

I think he eventually got home safely and sobered up quickly as well, I would imagine. Consider it a lesson well learned – you're going to get hurt if you play rough with the big boys.

Double-bungers were also very effective in a workplace situation.

Of the reported incidents I recall, some were downright dangerous but seemed to be readily accepted by the working community at large.

For years, many tried to emulate the cartoon characters at the movies by placing explosives under someone's chair and activating them secretly while the victim was sitting comfortably working at a desk – it was certainly a challenge, and I'm aware that it was carried out a few times, usually finishing in the sitting targeted person throwing the chair away post-explosion in some sort of retaliation.

At one place I worked, the buildings were typical of the age, including an old toilet which emanated from the pre-sewerage days where it was built outside in the yard well away from the main buildings for health and odour control reasons. To assist in the odour control and fresh air circulation, these buildings also had a ventilation gap of about two hundred millimetres at the top of the door and the same at the bottom.

Around cracker time of year, it became a common trick to wait till the target workmate was settled down on the toilet, then roll a lit bunger in under the bottom door gap. This was not always effective, as the target would expect it and the toilet seat being some five hundred millimetres back from the door provided plenty of time to react. The target usually either just kicked it back out, or placed their hefty work boots over the bunger, successfully extinguishing it or at least muffling the effect.

As always, where there is a problem, someone comes up with a solution.

Growing next to the toilet was a bamboo bush with canes of varying thickness. The trick was to select a very flexible piece, tape a bunger to the very end tip of it, light the bunger wick and then poke the stick under the door moving it rapidly from side to side and back and forth.

The control the attacker had was perfect because he could keep the bunger in such a position that the victim had to get off the seat to stamp it out, that's if they could catch it. All that was heard, in an attempt to extinguish the bunger, was the sound of boots stamping rapidly on the floor that sounded like a sort of weird frenzied dance, with a few words of abuse and finally an explosion. Then a long string of abusive words.

The next episode is not about double-bungers, but about a much more powerful explosive material.

Gelignite was used in the electricity supply industry for years when rock needed to be blasted to create a hole to stand power poles. It was also used to blast very large trees when mechanised saws were just not practical.

One depot in my employers group had a young apprentice called Peter who delighted in giving cheek to the more mature workers – two in particular. They in turn would retaliate by either roughing him up a bit or returning the abuse manyfold.

This particular day, he purposely set these two up and they retaliated as expected. He pretended to go a bit further with his temper and yelled at them, 'I'm sick of you two idiots – I'm gonna kill you both.'

The two stirrers, who worked together on a pole hole-boring machine, laughed off Peter's threat and started to drive out of the depot for the day's work in the field.

The truck the borer plant was mounted on was something like a ten-ton Austin or Morris truck that had a very slow but powerful low gear. The vehicle would crawl along on its own at an idle in this gear. I've heard of farmers using this facility when loading hay from the field onto one of these trucks; no driver was required during the loading process.

Peter had set the whole day up. He had meticulously made a replica stick of gelignite, complete with visible lookalike detonating material which he had loaded with powder from a double-bunger so it burnt just like a fuse. He admitted this bit was not all that real-looking but in the circumstances he had planned who stops to consider such a detail?

Running out from the depot building with said stick of lookalike gelignite in hand and fuse alight, and yelling his death threat, he jumped onto the truck's running board and threw the 'gelignite' through the window into the truck cabin, where it landed on the floor.

It looked real enough to the truck occupants and they both bailed out of the truck cabin with the truck in low gear and crawling slowly towards the depot's open gate and out to the street. To their credit, they yelled to everyone that the truck was about to explode and to get away from it.

Luckily for the passing street traffic the truck hit a pothole in the yard, altering the steering direction, and the truck now headed for one of the steel pipe gate posts. The truck nudged up against the post, bending it over, and then it stalled. End of drama one would think.

No, not really.

As with most good work stories, the boss has to be in the picture somewhere. Sure enough, the chief electrical engineer arrived at the depot at that point and looked at the scene that confronted him.

The borer truck had collided with the main gate post and looked like it had started to crawl up it, so damage to the truck underneath would be possible.

No other vehicles could get in or out of the depot yard because the borer was effectively blocking the gate.

The front gate post was bent badly so the gate couldn't close.

Two older staff members were chasing a second-year apprentice around the depot yard yelling abuse at him.

The rest of the depot staff were gingerly poking their heads out from safe hiding spots.

Two staff members were standing well back behind the borer truck with fire extinguishers at the ready.

Peter was severely reprimanded, as were the other two.

7

Kids Should Be Seen and Heard

Most of these stories have either been related to me by friends and or neighbours first hand over the years, or I have experienced them myself. I have included kids at ages from toddlers right up to teenagers. I believe the innocence of the younger brigade enhances the humour and is far more entertaining than any older group.

Henry, four years, and his sister of around three years, were chatting on the trampoline in their backyard near our adjoining fence where I was gardening. They both said good day to me and I joined in the conversation briefly before returning to my garden duties and they went on chatting to each other.

Their mother's demanding voice from the house caught my attention and broke up their chatting with, 'You two come inside now please – at once.'

The kids' response was no movement and continuation of chatting.

Mother, again, a few minutes later, 'You two better be in here by the time I count to ten.' She then started counting out loud.

The kids were obviously enjoying their chat and in immediate response Henry said to his sister with a sigh, 'Oh, I wish she could count to thirty like I can.'

On the other side of my yard we had another pair of developing leading citizens; where the conversation was centred around the four-year-old remarking to his older sister that he wished he was older so he could do things like she could – like stay up later at night and go to a real school and do other older kids' things.

His six-year-old sister had the answer. She said, 'To get to be older you have to have a birthday, you know, like when people sing happy birthday and stuff. I know what to do,' she said in an excited tone, 'I could sing that now and that will be a birthday for you and make you older.' She then wished him happy birthday and sang the happy birthday song all the way through – including a hip, hip, hooray at the end. Job done.

This one is from a family living on the edge of suburbia next to a nature reserve.

The five-year-old son was yelling from the backyard in a frantic voice, 'Dad. Dad.'

Fifteen seconds later again, 'Dad. Dad.'

From inside the house, Dad said in a gruff voice. 'Just a minute, son, I'm busy talking to your mother.'

A few more seconds passed and again the boy yelled, 'Dad. Dad.' after a pause and with no response, 'Well…Mum. Mum.'

After a few more minutes, Dad came out and gave the boy a rather lengthy, stern lecture on how communications things worked around there. 'When I said, "Just a minute, I'm busy," that means I heard you and I'd come out when I'm ready and not before – it means you then stop calling out and just wait until I come to you. You must not interrupt when people are talking to each other, it's very rude.'

Dad continued the lecture, 'It's not right for you to keep on yelling at me or your mother. You need to understand we have other things to do than just run after you every time you yell out. We also heard your little sister Susie scream. Did you two have a fight? Did you hurt her?'

'No, we didn't have a fight – I didn't hurt her,' was the boy's response.

'Well now, what's the problem?' asks Dad.

Boy's response, in a disappointed tone, 'It doesn't matter now.'

Dad enquired, 'What do you mean it doesn't matter now? It was very urgent a while ago.'

'Yeah, well that was when the lizard was still here,' the boy said.

Dad's voice took on a sound of urgency, 'Lizard? What lizard? Where is it now?'

The boy volunteered, 'It was a big brown one with spots and stripes. It was outside near the sliding screen door there when Susie came out to the backyard. She saw it and got frightened, that's why she screamed then ran out to the front garden.'

'Well, where's the lizard now?' asks Dad.

'I don't know. I suppose it's hiding somewhere,' responded junior.

'Well, did you see which way it went?' said Dad while frantically visually scanning the backyard.

'No, I couldn't see that from here,' says the boy.

'What do you mean you couldn't see where it went? You were standing here,' demanded Dad.

'Yes, but I couldn't see where it went, 'cause when Susie got frightened, she left the door open and it ran inside the house.'

'What? Why didn't you tell me then?' demanded Dad.

'I tried to a few times, but you said you were too busy, remember?' answered the boy.

At that point, there was a fearful scream from Mum inside the house, calling out hysterically to Dad, to get a horrible crawly thing out of there.

The boy called back to his mum, 'Dad can't come just now, Mum, because he's busy talking to me. Did you find the lizard?'

Mum said, 'How did you know there was a lizard in here? Did you put it in here? If you knew this thing was in here, why didn't you tell your father?' Followed by another brace of blood-curdling screams.

The boy's response was, "I tried to tell him, but he said he was too busy. But I think him and I must be finished talking, because he's running into the house now.'

After he got Mother settled down and out of the house, Father told me it took him the rest of the day to rid the house of the lizard, which was actually a very confused goanna close to a metre long.

It took an hour to find Susie, who had sought refuge in a neighbourhood friend's house. Poor little girl must have thought her backyard had turned into Jurassic Park and she was not going back there easily.

Dad was instructed by Mum to take the clothes off the clothesline as it looked like it was about to rain. Some of the items were still slightly damp and Dad wasn't sure whether to take them in or not as it appeared to him the suspected rain cloud was heading away from them.

The nine-year-old son was playing in the backyard and much closer to the open back door of the house, so Dad asked him to relay a question.

'Go and ask your mother if she wants me to take her jeans and track pants off the line now or leave them till later tonight.' He intended that the boy would actually go inside to do so, then return with the appropriate response.

The son, without moving position, yelled at the top of his voice, broadcasting to the immediate neighbourhood, 'Mum, Dad wants to know if you want him to take your pants off right now, or he thinks it would be better to do it later tonight?'

Albert, who was around seven and a half, and his sister Emily, just turned six, were engaged in running races in the backyard and, as always, Albert being older, made the rules. His most important rule was that he would start each race by counting to the go number – which, like Emily, I understood was usually one, two, and go on three. Albert apparently didn't like the common 'get set, get ready, go' system.

The first 'get set' was announced (by Albert of course) then one, two, three, and sister Emily took off.

But Albert said, 'No, you ran too early and that was a false start, so I win that race.'

Sister Emily said, 'You said three and I ran.'

Albert explained, 'But the go number this time was four.'

Emily asked how she was supposed to know that.

'You just have to wait till I say go,' explained Albert.

OK, Emily accepted the new amendment to the get-set-go rule.

Next race was starting and official starter Albert was on cue.

One, two, and Albert started running, yelling 'go' as he took off. Emily ran after him but Albert won the race.

Serious debate ensued again. This time, Emily was getting fairly well peeved with this Albert's Rules game and said she would call the numbers and the go for the next race. But Albert wouldn't have a bar of it – this race game was his idea and they had to play to his rules.

OK, Emily was up for one more shot at this athletic pursuit. They lined up. The Albert count started. One, two, three, four, and Emily guessed the go number this time would be five, so she took off running.

Albert called false start again, because the go number this time was seven. So he won again.

Sister Emily walked up to Albert – who was still expounding why he was the winner yet again – kicked him in the shins and walked inside. Albert yelled to his mother that Emily wouldn't play properly

Mother of course unaware of Albert's previous scams, told Emily to play properly with her brother.

Emily lined up again and the Albert countdown started. One, and Albert started running, yelling go and laughing mockingly. Emily was quick off the mark too and ran up the back of Albert and sort of tackled him by jumping on his back before he got into full stride. Albert fell heavily, copped a bleeding nose, a mouthful of grass and a badly damaged ego. Emily got up ran to the finish, claiming the race win.

Emily walked back inside past Mother, who asked was everything all right.

'Yes, Mum, I played properly with Albert – I played the game his way.'

'That's nice, dear. See how much better it is when we all get along. Where's Albert now?' enquired Mother.

Emily's response was, 'I think he's out there eating grass and he must have picked his nose because it's bleeding. He's been acting weird all day.'

Mum said, 'He's what?' and went to investigate.

This story was reported to me from the mother who carried out the resulting investigation into how Albert got a bleeding nose and grass stains on his only good school shirt.

The following came from an acquaintance of mine who had a good friend who owned a pie and pasty shop in eastern Sydney.

This owner grew tired of small children running everywhere in his shop yelling at the top of their voice and seemingly uncontrolled by the parents who took no notice. It was very upsetting for other customers. He was becoming paranoid about this behaviour. He recalled seeing an appropriate sign somewhere once and in a whimsical mood one day he had a similar one made and displayed in a prominent place for the parents to read, 'In This Shop All Well Behaved Children Are Always Welcome. The Rest Will Be Caught and Made Into Pies.'

He had hoped the parents of such annoying children might take the message as seriously as it was intended and control their children better. However, it seemed to have little effect, although he noticed most parents pointing the message out to their children and hopefully explaining the ramifications. The kids, however, called his bluff by still running everywhere.

The owner thought his next idea should have the desired effect. He made some special pies, which were put in a conspicuous place in his display case. They were made with a bit of moulded pastry cleverly fashioned into little fingers complete with fingernails, just protruding from under the lid on the edge of some pies. Obviously, it was designed to arrest the children's bad behaviour, but it stopped his regular customers instead. Most kids who saw these special pies and recalled the signs message ran screaming from the shop, with parents in close pursuit trying to calm them down.

The shop owner fielded a mountain of abuse from parents who shopped there, and much as he tried to explain his dilemma in attempting to avoid an accident in his shop, thereby protecting their kids, he was threatened with a massive customer walkout, so the kids finger pies were removed.

He took no further action on the problem for a few weeks. He then had another brain wave and installed another sign that read, 'Children Must Run Around The Shop Perimeter Three Times Before Being Served.'

The first of many parents complained that the shop owner couldn't tell their children what to do. One woman gave the owner a severe dressing down. 'That requirement on the sign is ridiculous. It's offensive. How dare you instruct my children to do anything. What is wrong with you? My children will be served when they want something and they won't be running around just to please you and your stupid wacky sign.'

And they didn't.

There is no doubt, we human beings are a strange lot.

A young dad (no, not me), had a peculiar habit of every time he drove the family past a pub he would sing his version of the ABC *Play School* theme song – you know the one: There's a bear in there, and a chair as well…'

The version he preferred went something like this:

> 'There's a beer in there
> And a chair as well
> Lots of great mates

With stories to tell
It's open wide
So come inside
And play pool.'

His wife protested every time but he persisted every time they drove past a pub, especially his local pub. Four-year-old son Johnny got to learn it perfectly – Dad's lyrics, that is. And Dad would encourage the kids to sing along, seemingly just to upset Mother.

Johnny was singing it to himself at his early learning school one day. Overhearing it, the teacher recognised the tune and understood it to be the real *Play School* theme song; she was impressed, so she asked Johnny to sing his song for the group. And Johnny did.

The note that was sent home with Johnny was a bit upsetting for his mother, but was extremely upsetting for Dad when he arrived home that night faced with Mother's wrath.

An older child's story. A child who should have known better.

On a field trip to the Australian War Memorial in Canberra, the group of thirteen- and fourteen-year-old boy students were receiving a lecture in the World War II display area. One student, we'll call him George, had no interest in the lecture and his mind wandered with more interest to some of the actual displays – especially the different types of big guns. His body followed his mind in its wandering.

It was time for all the groups to move on to the next exhibition hall and George was given the hurry up by a fellow student, 'Come on, we have to go.'

George, standing at the front of the barrel of a rather large gun with his school blazer over the end of the barrel, replied quietly that he couldn't move anywhere, as he had got his arm stuck right up to the elbow, in the barrel of the gun. I'm told it was one of the howitzer type used in World War II.

His mate asked a reasonable question. 'Why did you put your arm in there in the first place?'

A not so reasonable answer was, 'Just to see if it would fit.'

George had obviously paid no attention to the lecture, as he missed the bit on how barrels of guns have internal rifling or spiral grooving to spin the projectile it fired, thereby assisting in range and accuracy. By panicking and trying to pull his arm straight out, he was going against the rifling grooves which he hadn't realised assisted in getting his arm inserted in the first place, and subsequently he tore quite a lot of skin off his bare arm during the eventual extraction.

His classmates gave poor George heaps of stirring over this for some time – he was even accused of trying to bring home an unofficial World War II souvenir under his school blazer.

One can only wonder what the War Memorial cleaners must have thought when they came across a World War II gun with bits of human flesh on the pointing end of it.

Nightmare in the Museum all over again for George.

While on the subject of older kids who should have known better, here's one from the dim but not so dark past of yours truly.

As a young whippersnapper of around fourteen, I joined the cool group trying out cigarette smoking – unbeknown to my parents of course. Our toilet was situated down the back of the yard and that's where I would go to have a few puffs of the fags.

The toilet was, as in all towns before sewerage services, a bucket/can pan system and the local council provided a regular collection and replacement can service.

It was a perfect place as it wasn't frequented regularly, with only a small household, and the ventilation gaps in the door provided no evidence of smoking odour after I had left. The door faced away from the house, so no smoke clouds were evident either.

An accepted health practice in those days in an attempt to prevent the development of any nasty bugs or disease was to regularly pour kerosene into the pan, which would float and form a protective barrier on the top. Some people were very generous with the amount of kero pour and my family certainly subscribed to the practice.

This particular visit, I needed to actually use the toilet and made myself comfortable on the seat. What a perfect time for a fag, so I lit up and as normal, to hide the evidence, I placed the match into the toilet pan between my legs.

However, this time I must have still had some flame on the match

when I slipped it between my legs as the whole thing burst into flames. I quickly realised the kerosene was there. It started to burn the wooden seat and I removed that. There was a distinct smell of burning hair – mine. Panic ruled and I thought the kero could burn for quite a while – what could I do to put it out?

My father was planning to build an extension onto the adjacent garage and he had a pile of builder's sand stored just outside the toilet door. That would do it, I thought. I'll douse it with sand. Which I did.

A week later, my father came home one afternoon telling a story I could immediately relate to. He was asked by the man who collected the toilet pans, 'What the hell are you people eating at your house – I could hardly lift that pan of yours last week. That's the heaviest any of my staff have ever experienced.'

My parents couldn't work it out, but I thought maybe being half full of sand would have had something to do with the complained increase in weight.

8

Retirement, Ageing and Other Forms of Self-destruction

Our children are now middle-aged adults. It's a disturbing awakening when your oldest starts talking about their retirement plan.

Retirement? I've just finished successfully fighting off retirement and reluctantly but gracefully accepted the semi-retirement status.

The term 'semi-retirement' informs everyone you have voluntarily (and it's very important to include the voluntary word) decided that you are available if someone wants to consult you on whatever they are doing and or are having issues with, but you'll only do it if you really want to – it's not as if you have been fretting for something like this to come along. This demeanour you have adopted and made known to all covers the fact that, in reality, probably no one wants to permanently employ someone your age anyway, but it's comforting and reassuring to adopt this aloof attitude from here to the grave.

Of course there is always the nagging ruminated feeling that the industrial world is either heading in the wrong direction or stalled; it must be stalled, because no one has asked you to show them the way forward recently.

I believe this post-retirement/semi-retirement unwanted in the workforce feeling disappears fairly quickly. My guess with me is that, given my desire to still be part of it, it should happen around the ninety years of age mark – but it could be longer for some people.

My body is about ten years behind what the mind wants it to do. I get rather excited some mornings when the body is feeling great and I think it may be catching up to the mind and the whole unit can operate as one. But alas, by mid-morning, the body seems to realise what the mind is trying to do to it, and it retaliates violently by losing interest in the whole concept.

A few years ago at a family gathering, my wife asked our children to talk me into retiring all together, to just sit back and watch the world go by.

My eldest son said, 'Mum, if Dad retires, I'm never coming home again. He will be impossible to put up with. Retirement will drive him mad and anyone around him will suffer accordingly.'

His belief that I will still be busy doing something (that I think worthwhile) on the day I die, has prompted his plan to have my mobile phone included in my coffin and he will call the phone, activating the loudest ring tone and volume he can set it on, at the appropriate juncture during the funeral service.

He wants me to pre-record a greeting message, if time permits, saying, 'I can't take your call right now as I'm travelling, but please leave a message and I'll try and get back to you as soon as I know where I'vel ended up and what service is available.'

My wife absolutely hates the idea and has forbidden it. However, my

son, although he has always tried to comply with the wishes of his parents, said, 'Mum, there are times when a man must do what a man must do – to do what is in his heart.'

Sitting back watching the world go by reminds me of a great old friend of mine who decided to do just this. Harry and his wife moved out of the city and bought a small landholding with a lovely old cottage in a country town. The plan worked well, with them both kicking back enjoying retirement and the peace and tranquillity of the bush.

Harry and his wife bought a 'Jack & Jill' outdoor setting and when the weather suited, they would spend a lot of time enjoying a cool drink in the summer evenings sitting side by side in the Jack & Jill under a beautiful old elm tree in their backyard.

However, as the years went on, the furniture got the worse for wear with weather damage and Harry's regular spilling of his cool drinks and cigarette burns on the table section between the seats. From then on, in the off season, Harry would always take the furniture piece to his secluded workshop shed and restore it completely; fix it up ready for the next spring and summer. His secluded workshop was a no-go area for anyone else – it was Harry's get away place.

Given Harry's increasing sloppiness, the nagging from his Jill also became more intense and Harry wondered at the end of this last season just how much more the nagging was likely to increase, as it was now nowhere near as enjoyable as it used to be under the old elm tree. With his every move in the last few seasons he was being warned, 'Don't spill that drink again. Put that Esky on the ground. Move your drink away from my side. Don't put your cigarette there, the smoke is a terrible smell; now you've set fire to the newspaper again,' and so on. This wasn't the kicking back retirement he had planned.

Harry renovated the furniture piece in the off season once again and coming into late spring he installed it outside in the same place under the elm as always. However, he needed to modify the site somewhat this time as the renovations made the unit a bit different.

As always, his Jill came out to see the result and set up for the first date of the season.

He had rejuvenated the two seats in the same quality manner as always – but being a fairly resourceful man, the adjoining centre table section was now two metres long between the seats, complete with its own new sturdy legs to support an Esky full of stubbies on his end, an extra large built-in ashtray and an optional spring-loaded divider screen closer to Jill's end that he could deploy at will from his seat.

Harry told me his Jill didn't like the new look Jack & Jill piece one little bit and after all the effort he had put into the renovation, he was disappointed.

Briefly on the subject of alcoholic drinks, and the increased effect of over indulgence as you get older.

I'm not certain how many people are aware that red wine was invented by the devil – my reasoning is that in my experience a hangover from that stuff threatens to last forever, takes away your power of reasoning, eliminates any earlier beliefs you once held surrounding your going to heaven. You seem to converse with the opposite side by saying things like 'Why the hell did I drink so much?' and 'That was a hell of a night.' Your immediate fondest wish is just to die and it prepares you for any punishment available in hell when you eventually decide nothing could be worse than the way you currently feel – not even the damnation of hell. It gives you a realistic sample of what to expect.

However, beer on the other hand is an invention from the heavenly angels, as it seems to bring people closer to God. With a hangover from beer, at least you can still think clearly, as I have heard so many such people seem to earnestly pray, 'Please, God, make my gut stop rumbling and take this headache away' – and the prayer eventually (usually) does work in the same lifetime.

Some other observations also come to mind where increased age has a noticeable effect.

You know you're getting older when you look to match your restaurant menu selection – especially the sauce – with the colour of the clothes you're wearing. No matter how carefully you place your napkin, the sauce still either gets past it or through it. You take much care to avoid this and when it still happens you look at what colour food the person at the next table is eating and suspect he must have flicked it your way when you weren't looking.

Another sign in the ageing process where you need to take more care, I've noticed, is the simple task of tying the cord of your track pants or shorts. I obviously haven't mastered it completely yet, as it doesn't matter how cautiously I arrange the knot when tying, when the toilet urgency arises, I invariable pull the wrong bit and end up with a new knot that a master mariner not only couldn't recognise, but couldn't untie.

I think every household has a safe place – the place where you keep what you consider are valuable items. We're not talking cash, jewellery, our last will and testament or the deeds to the house, or life insurance documents – we're talking about real everyday treasures.

You hear older people remark when looking for one of these treasures, 'I know I put it in a safe place, but I just can't quite recall where that is right now.'

One of the biggest traps with safe places is when you change the location for any reason – could be because you think someone else like a burglar might find your safe place; you have a tradesman coming to do some work in that area; or you think of an even safer place; or you actually forgot where the original safe place is – or you, let's say, just temporally misplaced it. So when new valuable stuff comes along, you have to find another safe place.

At the moment in our initial safe place, in particular, we think we have instruction manuals for any number of can't-live-without appliances that we have been using very well for years, but now one of them is not doing what its supposed to do and we're sure the instructions will have the answer in the Frequently Asked Questions section.

It's important that we find a manual, for this model number no longer appears on the internet. And the current local retailer rep for this brand says, 'It's a what? What does it do? Sorry, never heard of it, sir. How old did you say it is?'

This safe place could also hold the address book with the contact details of all our relatives and friends who we send Christmas cards to (sometimes); photos of importance; various menus from many of the local home delivery takeaway restaurants; a number of service booklets from funerals we have attended (just in case we want to pinch one of the hymns for ours); items that we didn't want to throw out but don't know where else to put them; the handwritten recipe for that fantastic dish a relative gave us and we're not game to ask for it again, thereby admitting we lost it originally; and I'm sure a lot of other valuables.

And then, a real joyful Christmas-morning-like moment happens, when we unexpectedly find our safe place, while we were looking for something else. It was located in the weirdest location, prompting us to say to each other, 'No wonder we couldn't find it – what a stupid location for a safe place.'

But then the unbridled rapture fades quickly when we discover that most of the things we thought were safely kept in this safe place are not there.

Now where did we put them? We know we put them in a safe place. So that means we have another safe place somewhere. It starts you thinking you could have a safe place in every room in the house.

I have suggested that, if and when we next find any of the safe places, we immediately put a note in them to tell us where the other safe places are located. And then when we go to the other safe places to renew our acquaintances with the contents there, we should gather them all up and just resort to having the one safe place.

But hang on a minute, that's how this whole safe place thing started in the first place.

Another don't-attempt exercise in your declining years is trying to be a smart-arse with people much younger. An example: I walked into my usual barbers and when my turn came, I sat in the chair as always.

The young barber greeted me, placed the clothes protector cloak on me and asked the same old question, 'What will it be today then?'

I have been going to this barber for close to five years, getting the same ordinary haircut and being asked this same silly question every time.

This day, I thought I'd change it around a bit. 'What'll it be today? I know: make me look young and handsome,' I said in a smug sarcastic manner.

The barber was quick to the response and said as he pulled the cloak off me, 'Oh, I'm sorry sir, you have the wrong shop. The Magic Castle is two doors up.'

Chalk one up for the barber.

Generally, it's my conviction that most sensible and reasonable people have disappeared. The majority of people I deal with day to day in business have graduated from the School of Stupid, with honours, and with a major in the study of Applied Lazy.

I believe the virtually small percentage of good ones who are left in the workforce are keeping the whole country ticking over and that must be somewhat of a daunting job for them. And it is so delightful when I come across such a person in a conversation or through a business dealing. It is decidedly rewarding and memorable.

I may be alone on this point, but it appears to me that effective communication and a proactive approach at all levels is also on the scrap heap; governments of all political persuasion in all jurisdictions have set and agreed on the standard for this.

Based on my experience, I'm setting a scenario below as a typical example to emphasise my point.

When we as a community recognise a problem that makes our community less liveable, we take it to the particular state or territory government who in turn says it's a national issue consequently the federal government is the body to handle it.

The feds in turn eventually form some sort of fact-finding working group to study whether it really is a problem. This working group is usually headed by a 'political friend' of the government. A few months down the track, the working group is eventually formed.

First move is that the working group encourages the continuation of the problem, just so they as a group can study it first hand for a designated time frame to get a full understanding and appreciation of why we are in this reported undesirable situation.

Another few months passes and the working group officially state they have had good effective deliberations about the issue and recognised there is a problem nationally. Good progress is being made. However, they need more funding.

The feds say the state and territory governments have to put some funds in and they in turn respond with the argument that it's a federal government issue. Consequently, no funding from the states and territories is offered.

However, while they recognise it should be a federal government funded project, they do feel strongly that they should have a say in the deliberations of the working group as the results and findings will affect them and their communities.

Consequently, some more months later the working group reports they have received formal requests from all but two of the state and territory governments, who now demand to be part of this group. This new development now has to go back to the federal government, through the minefield of the bureaucratic process and eventually to the appropriate minister.

The federal government minister says he will only consider the request valid if all the state and territory governments are behind it – the minister demands a total accord before giving it any further consideration at all. Emphasising the point, the minister indicates his reasoning that, given two of the states are not keen to be on board, there is a lack of national support, so the problem can't be as widespread as first thought. For the minister, this poses the question whether the federal government really need to manage the issue when, on the face of what has now transpired, each state and territory that believes they have this problem should deal with it accordingly.

Federal cabinet agrees and the working group is disbanded after their three years of sitting, but not before an official report is tabled for the federal minister indicating that the working group has effectively carried out their allotted task, their responsibilities have been met and they are subsequently officially congratulated in Parliament. Hear. hear. A job well done.

But each of the state and territory governments don't want to deal with the issue alone as (given that two of them don't want to touch it) the rest will either do it each separately (that's six times differently in total), or band together, thereby pooling resources and do it just the once. But isn't that last option what federation was about originally?

So the community may well be stuck with the problem until one of the charities decides to fix it.

I defy anyone to convince me that this above scenario can't happen in our present political and corporate environment. This is so ridiculous, it could be thought as being from a *Yes, Minister* script, which was purposely designed to be humorous. But it's not from any TV show script – sadly it's our own reality.

As I made reference to above, good conversation, good manners and respect are nearly all gone. It's probably somehow related to the above school of thought among other rationales, and that electronic gadget that seems stitched to people's hands telling them how to live and how to think. There is little need to hone the skill of conversation – hardly anyone uses it anyway. As long as the texting fingers are working, that's all that's needed now.

A person with a young male voice from one of those annoying marketing call centres called me one day recently; he gave his cover away immediately and I said I wasn't interested in what he had to offer. He wouldn't acknowledge my comments, interrupting me by rabbiting on with the product promo, and I hung up on him.

Five seconds later, the phone rang again and it was the same person, who said in a gruff voice, 'Did you just hang up on me?' I was astounded, as I thought they would get quite used to that in that vocation.

I said, 'Yes, and if you wait around a second, here it comes again.'

I couldn't believe it – he actually called back again the third time and he got the same treatment. Being that thin-skinned, and with no conversation skills – just the ability to talk but not listen – he is obviously in the wrong job. Fancy a marketing call centre person complaining about my telephone etiquette.

Genuine Good Samaritans have disappeared – they'll now help you up with one hand and rob you with the other. Or is that governments? I get con artists, crooks and some politicians mixed up for some reason. Oh, I remember now how to tell the difference: one won't show their face in public and the other always shows their face in public.

My good, best clothes (we're talking funeral attending attire here), are apparently, well, years out of date. And one of my grandkids said they were, 'Downright dowdy, Pop.'

'Dowdy?' I screamed, 'Dowdy?' A bit out of date would have sufficed. 'Well, what do you call *me* then?'

I'll remember his response forever. 'I'll let you work on that one alone, Pop,' as he returned to his mobile phone game, with something of a smirk on his young face.

Of course, the next serious step past getting older is death. This came from a good friend – the son of an old man on his last days.

The local priest was called by the family to the deathbed of their father, an old man well known in the community for his grouchy and offensive behaviour – we'll call him Oscar. Given that Oscar had never attended church, the priest offered him an opportunity to unburden himself of any sins or inappropriate behaviour as part of the reflection on his life. The priest asked him if he had any misgivings or sorrows for his life that he would like to discuss.

'Yes, Father, I do have some regrets,' the dying man said.

The priest asked Oscar if he would like to share his thoughts.

'Well, all right, if you must be so bloody intrusive, I should have been a lot more aggressive and belligerent, more critical of others. I should have displayed a better form of negativity and insults and I should have told a lot more people how much I hated them.' He paused, took a gasping shallow breath and continued, 'Also, I think I might not have got around to telling some people I know just how bloody stupid they are – and they should be told, because the way they carry on, they obviously don't know.'

The priest wasn't sure how to tell Oscar that he had nothing to regret in this area of his life – he had certainly excelled well in all things mentioned.

Oscar continued, 'Because when I started to get old, people thought I had mellowed and they started to show kindness and sympathy towards me and I just couldn't retaliate properly. My thinking got so slow that I couldn't think of the right words to tell them off with until after they were gone. That's probably my biggest sorrow. But talking to you now, Father, has seemed to bring that sharpness back for some things,' Oscar said in a lighter tone.

'I'm glad I've brought you some joy at this time, Oscar,' responded the priest, momentarily delighted that he might have changed Oscar's outlook on the world at this his darkest hour.

'Yes,' said Oscar, 'you have been very helpful. It just takes a bit longer now for all the pieces to fall into place. You see, I never wanted you here at all. It was my interfering, do-gooder family who called you – but now I'm happy to be able to tell you what I should have said when you first came in. Now piss off, you Bible-bashing hypocrite. I'm happy you stayed around long enough for me to recall what I really think of you – you're a money-hungry, interfering, bloodsucking bastard. Now get out.'

The priest said in disappointed tone, 'I'm glad I could be of some assistance for you. Oscar.' He shuffled out with his head bowed to report the conversation to the grieving family.

There are many advantages to being of the older generation set – somewhere in between the official generation classifications of the Builders and the Baby Boomers.

One important advantage, and probably the most important one, is that I have so many memories, a smidgeon of which I have submitted in this book, and I'm so thankful that I can still recall the pertinent details. This is nothing short of a blessing, as many of my friends at this age, and even much younger, do not enjoy the satisfaction of accurate recollection. I believe some of the underpinning for this retentiveness is being able to keep that 'funny bone' in my head in tune at all times.

Look after your cerebral funny bone, keep it well nourished and in tune through observation and consideration, and you will hopefully appreciate the best humour that life not only can, but does, offer.

www.ingramcontent.com/pod-product-compliance
Lightning Source LLC
Chambersburg PA
CBHW030915080526
44589CB00010B/319